MW01291196

BUDDHISM FOR BEGINNERS:

The incredible book that will definitively change your perspective on Buddhism and Zen Meditation

by

Gregory F. George

CONTENTS

Introduction to meditation

Zen says "When I'm hungry, I eat. When I'm tired, I sleep". But you have to do it conscientiously, without getting carried away by the events. Zen is a daily consciousness, as Matsu said. [1]

Without getting carried away by events. A phrase by Fabrizio De Andrè comes into my mind: "Continuerai a farti scegliere o finalmente sceglierai?"[2](Will you continue to make you choose, or will you finally choose?)

I will often make analogies between the two cultures, not only to show differences and similarities, but to show what's missing in our actions to be Zen.

You will find many pop references. Both because of what I've just written, and to make your reading more enjoyable. You will also find not really pop references, because they are part of my cultural background and in this book you'll find also personal experiences. I decided to write them because I think some of life lived notes and anecdotes can make reading more enjoyable. And also because it is thanks to my experience and my cultural background that I've been able to write this book, and it is through your experience and your cultural baggage that you will understand it and approach Zen. In conclusion you will also find a few tales.

There will also be references to Greek philosophy. Listen to the words of Robert M. Piercing [3]

"In this book there is a lot of talk about the way of seeing things typical of the ancient Greeks."[4]. Well, I am not the first to combine Zen and Philosophy. This *auctoritas* comforts me.

Part 1

Definitions, questions and answers

Let's begin by trying to contextualize Zen, and to give it a smattering to those who do not know anything about it.

What is Zen? The monk and Socrates

One does not learn to play the organ from those who build the organs, but from those who play them.

[Galileo Galilei]

What is Zen? What are its doctrinal principles? It is easy to answer the first question. It is a meditation practice that comes from the Buddhist religion, indeed, it is within the Buddhist religion. It is less easy to answer the second question. In fact, it has no doctrine in a metaphysical and transcendent sense, and refers to those of Buddhism. It has rules and practices that have only one purpose: happiness here and now. Not only in the sense that it does not give importance to paradisiacal comforting ideas of a life after death, but also in that which doesn't think too much about the future. Here and now, but right here and now, in this instant and in this place. With the advantage that this action made *hic et nunc*, we will benefit for a long time. Another very important thing is that we can make practically all the actions of our day, or at least a good part, zen. All things will shine with a new light. In some cases, they will just start to shine, from opaque they were.

Zen must be practiced, not understood. Perhaps it is for this reason that for us Westerners, at least at the beginning, may seem difficult. Socrates used to walk around the streets of Athens asking "what is it?" He was looking for the essence, not for descriptions. He proudly defined himself as the gadfly. He was a little annoying, according to what he got there. A Buddhist monk would have answered him with silence, and make him do Zen practices, explaining them. Moreover, when the monks meditate, they must also bear insects.

When Zen was born?

According to the Treccani Encyclopedia, between the Twelfth and the Thirteenth Century.[5] But the situation is not so simple: here's what the Zen Rome website reports:

Zen, which literally means meditation, has ancient origins dating back 5,000 years. Practiced in the pre-Aryan civilization in India, it was rediscovered by the Buddha as a vehicle to access a dimension of wisdom and spirituality.[6]

So, in practice?

For this reason, the Chinese tradition of Chán is also sometimes called *Zen*, but also the *Sòn* Korean and *Thiền* Vietnamese traditions. "*Zen* points directly to the human mind-heart, look at your true Nature and become Buddha."

The Bodhidharma definition of Zen:

A special transmission outside the scriptures
No dependence upon words and letters
Direct pointing at the soul of man
Seeing into one's nature and the entertainment of Buddhahood.

(*Four Sacred Verses of Bodhidharma*)

Who was Bodhidharma[7]

He was a Persian Buddhist monk who lived between the 5th and 6th centuries AD. According to tradition, he was the twenty-eighth heir to an unbroken line of descending directives from the Buddha..[8]

Who can practice Zen?

Zen is not an abstruse thing for Buddhist monks and weird Westerners, as we can all be Zen. It is not necessary to be Buddhists or fanatical of the East. I certainly am neither one nor the other, yet every day I find a way to do Zen practices because I like them and doing that makes me feel good. Moreover, a practice that is so little conceptual, can only be within everyone's reach. Therefore, whether you are an atheist, a Catholic, a Buddhist, etc., do it without hesitation. If you don't believe me, read here.

It is possible to show in a well-founded way, that the Zen exercise does not distance the exerciser from Christ, as feared by someone, but makes him find the way to be in him, a way to concretely experience the binomial "Christ-in-me "And" I-in-Christ. [...]Those who participate in the Zen exercises, or what is proposed in Europe under this name or other similar ones, are generally people who come from the "Western"cultural sphere. They can be Christians more or less deeply inserted into their religious beliefs; or non-baptized people who are looking for a religious point of view. The reaction to these exercises is different, and depends on the origin of each one. Simply rejecting the Zen exercise is totally inappropriate, as well as considering it dangerous and always warning against it. Not every medicine helps and helps everyone.[9]

In short, Zen does not nail you up and does not claim exclusivity.

As for your lifestyle, you certainly won't have to upset it. Once the meditation is over, you will return to normal, but Zen will have a very positive influence on your daily routine [10]. So much, that you probably won't find it monotonous anymore.[11]

What is the etymology of the word Zen?

The word Zen derives from the Japanese pronunciation of a Chinese character, that in Middle Chinese is pronounced d͡ziɛn. According to other hypotheses, instead, Zen derives from the Korean Seon, which derives from the Chinese Chan, which derives from the pali Dhana which indicates the practice of meditation.

I was undecided whether to insert this part or not. The thing that matters most to me, is that you can grasp the essence of Zen, and learn to practice it by gaining concrete advantages in your everyday life. Never mind if you don't know, or don't remember the etymology or the history of Zen, at least from the point of view of this book.

Because even those who have not read Freud can live a hundred years, as Rino Gaetano sings in "Mio fratello è figlio unico". If you want to live well, the most important thing is that you live in a Zen way.

Are there several Zen schools, or just one?

There are three of them and they are called Obaku, Rinzai and Soto.

The Rizai is more austere and therefore it became the favorite of the Samurai.[12]

What do the different Zen schools have in common?

First of all, the zazen, which is the meditation practice. Then, the fact of giving less attention to the study of sutras. Thirdly, the attention to detail when it comes to the transmission of the "lineage".

What is a sutra?

In Brahmanism, a sutra is a sacred text that transmits a teaching. In Buddhism, the sutras are the Buddha's sermons collected by the disciples after his death. Sutra is a Sanskrit term and means wire.[13]

What is the purpose of Zen?

The purpose of Zen is awareness. Awareness of what? Awareness that we do not coincide with our thoughts. Awareness that almost everything we have is not necessary. Awareness that our "I" is illusory, because, like all phenomena, it is transient and apparent. A Zen story speaks of cookies of different shapes, but all cut from the same cloth.

We must not escape from bad things, because we must learn to deal even with the negative and difficult components of life. Zen wants to teach us that even negative episodes can be useful, and if we can learn from them, they will strengthen us.

Who makes zen does not perform miracles, but manages to fully live the present moment despite all adversities.

What is the main obstacle?

The main obstacle is our ego.

*In order to know oneself, first of all it is important to separate what we are from our **ego**, that is the **false identity** that practically every person has developed by growing up. Our mind is continually dominated by endless thoughts of **self-centeredness**, greed, attachment, anger, pride, envy, etc.*

The ego is always lurking, and it is the cause of most suffering, as well as food for the monkey mind. It is essential to be aware of his presence to understand that you are not your thoughts.[14]

How do we reach awareness?

Through meditation.

What can't Zen do?

Zen cannot make suffering disappear, but it helps us to accept it. Awareness also concerns the negative things in life and, above all, suffering. Zen helps us to accept it. Attention: not to resign ourselves, but to set our life based on them. Suffering can help us shed light on our relationships with others. Attention bis: it is useless to remove it, because sooner or later it comes back, but it is not that we have to look for it. We must accept suffering without feeling guilty and without accusing anyone. We must accept suffering knowing that life is loved despite the things that make us feel bad. We must accept suffering, knowing that we are not suffering even if it is part of us. We must help those who are suffering, and try to soothe everyone's pain.

Furthermore, Zen does not make us have mystical or extrasensory visions. But it can make us have insight, which is an immediate restructuring of the understanding of reality. It does not derive from a series of arguments, but, indeed, from an intuition. An example of insight is that of Newton's apple.

What is the difference between detachment and non-attachment?

Detachment indicates a desire not to have, or not to do something. Non-attachment means letting things happen and reaching us, without fretting us too much in case of loss (so let's enjoy them!). Zen supports non-attachment.

In short, we can also live without them. In the face of any objection, we clarify that no one, not even Zen, takes theft or loss of money lightly. But the point is that according to Zen, our happiness should not depend on them.

Similarly, for the desire to have new goods. A Mass is sung "Search first the Kingdom of God and his justice and all the rest will be given to you more". The Zen states "seek the richness that is within you, and welcome all the remaining pleasurable things that will come to you". I remember a version of Latin that spoke of a city on fire, destroyed/at the mercy of enemies and one [15] that replied "omnia mecum porto" (I take all my belongings with me, that is to say my wisdom and my culture) to those who were surprised to see it peaceful and calm despite the huge losses. Don't you find it a little Zen?

Seneca spoke of the firmness of the essay that remains unperturbed at external events, because it draws from within itself its own strength and awareness of its own value.

He was a little zen too. Moreover, every wise person who is aware of his own value has a hint of Zen in him or better, he shares some values of Zen without being aware of it.

Why does Zen seem difficult?

Probably, because it has no intellectual or cognitive approach.[16] The Japanese use the expression "I shin den shin", which we could translate as "from heart to heart". Zen masters do not explain, Zen masters show. We are referring to all activities related to Zen. And when they show, the disciples cannot ask questions.[17] The disciple learns by looking for years at what the teacher is doing, especially in gestures. All this must take place in silence.

Part 2

Meditation

There are different types of meditation. We will only see a few. All of them have an element in common and it is breathing.[18]

Cross-legged meditation and other types of meditation

The legs take the so-called position of the lotus, while the closed eyes serve to meet the frequency of 8-13 hertz, which is the alpha rhythm, that is the rhythm that allows us to disconnect from the external world, easily reachable by a non-stressed person.[19]

The position one assumes when one sits down to meditate is called zazen.[20]

The term *zazen* indicates precisely the posture of the Buddha.[21]

We must keep our eyes closed or half-closed to prevent the mind from being distracted by the outside world. The mind looks a bit like a monkey, it is a phrase that often occurs in the Zen world.

Koan Meditation

One type of meditation is called koan. Yes part by breathing three times, and it is best to do it using your belly. We inhale deeply and breathe out slowly and prolongedly. While we do it, we count from one to ten. Each breath corresponds to a number. It must be done ten times, from one to ten. If we distract ourselves, we must start from one. Koan meditation is one of the first things that Zen monks face, but it is also useful for the laity as it develops firmness and stability, two determining elements when making a decision. Furthermore, it helps us to maintain concentration.

Koan meditation uses koans, which are paradoxes.[22]

Shikantaza meditation has its clear rules. It is practiced by monks all over the world, and we can do it ourselves. The word shi means to cease, but we can translate it with tranquility, stillness. The word Kan we can translate it with awareness.[23] Taza indicates sitting in the simplicity of life.

Shikantaza meditation should be done in silence by contemplating external phenomena (but not their visual image), without interfering with them. We must not only be silent, but stop thoughts. We observe things and events and we keep the ego at bay. Let's go to shikantaza meditation in the most peaceful place possible, with the right light, with the right temperature, away from unpleasant odors, and maybe with some essence. In short, nothing should disturb us. Don't do it when we're tired and when we're weighed down.

The ideal would be to sit on a round cushion, the so-called zafu, placed on a blanket, and turn against the wall in order to have as few distractions as possible.

In theory we should put ourselves in the lotus position, but crossing our legs will suffice. The eyes must be half-open and set a point below us by about forty-five degrees. Better not to keep them closed completely, to avoid the risk of falling asleep. Let's take a first breath by sucking in very deep, and bring it to the abdomen. After that, let's exhale involving the pelvis and the whole lower part. In this way we are laying the foundations of our meditation. Let's repeat it three times. Let's move on to the second type of breath type. Also in this case, inspiring we will bring the breath to the abdomen, but exhaling we will expand the breath in the central part of the body. We do it to open the bust, to straighten the back, to relax energy and emotions. Let's do it twice. The third way of breathing is that the exhalation takes place in the upper part of the body, but also in the whole body, in order to feel ourselves totally present. All this will give us calm and stability.

Breathing must be abdominal, and must be done with the mouth closed, with the nostrils, calmly and silently. We do not force the rhythm of breathing, but let it flow naturally. We should hardly think we're breathing. Let thoughts flow freely, without suppressing or suffocating them, but neither without trying to capture them or understand them. In short, let's not give it too much importance. The same is true for sensations, both for positive and negative ones: let us accept them and not reject them. If they are positive, let's enjoy them but don't stick to them.

Shikantaza breathing must last at least a quarter of an hour / twenty minutes, but it is not forbidden to last even all evening. After all, we just have to sit and do nothing, in silence.

Thanks to shikantaza we will rediscover the awareness of our unity with the rest of the Universe. A unity that has always existed and for which we only needed to become aware.

No one forces us to meditate, and we can stop doing it whenever we want.

After the shikantaza meditation the four vows can be recited like the Zen monks do.[24]

The Pebble Meditation

It is simple and can be done by everyone, even by children. Indeed, it can be a fun way to introduce them to meditation. It can be done either alone or in company. They take pebbles and put them next to each other. He takes one in his hand and meditates on a sentence, breathing adequately.[25]

Other types of meditation

A new day[26]

Let's start right from the beginning, that is to say from awakening. Buddhist monks wake up when it is still dark, and enter the new day with the sun. But we don't need that much, of course. On the other hand, we can do a Zen meditation since awakening.

The same awakening can set us well towards meditation, being almost propaedeutic. It is recommended that it be done with a sweet and harmonious sound. It is also advised not to postpone waking up with the timeless "five more minutes" and if we really can't do without it when we decide that it's time to officially wake up let's do it with the right attitude and above all in a correct way. Certainly, a correct way is Zen. That will please even the laziest because it does not force us to get out of bed too abruptly and suddenly.

Yes part with breathing. We will do meditation while breathing. First we will direct the meditation towards the neck. The neck is important because it supports the head, the seat of the mind. We will then move on to the back, abdomen, pelvis, legs and finally feet, each with its own role and importance in our lives.

Remember we talked about Kill Bill's bride? I would like to imagine that his moving feet are just one of the last moments of a correct awakening, but then I remember that the journey to the East and the learning of the techniques are later, and could not have been otherwise. However, even so we see the centrality of this part of our body.

At this point we open our eyes, observe the environment that surrounds us and let it enter the world with us on this new day.

Every day, for Zen it can be the day. A special day full of surprises and opportunities. Even before knowing Zen, I started the day with the motivational phrase: I don't know what will happen to me today. It's not so strange that I have approached this practice, right?

It is not certain that the day reserves only for us beautiful things, and to face this risk I have adopted another mantra that recites: anything goes. Even negative experiences can be useful again, if only in terms of growth. Admitted then that they are really negative, and that in the long run they do not prove to be, on the contrary, the condition of moments of possibility.

Thanks to breathing and these two mantras I can now start the day full of energy. Actually, I need other things to start loading, but let's say I'm already well prepared. The first is the physical contact of the feet (still them!) With the floor, the domestic symbol of the mother earth.

My floor is cold. A cold of tiles. If yours is warm, because having the carpet or the parquet, it's ok anyway.

At this point, the ablutions. It is not just a hygienic question, but a need to feel the water running over you, to wake up and to relax.

Now, breakfast. The beauty of Zen is that it tells us to eat what we like, without too many healthy moralisms. But he tells us what to do. Indeed, above all what not to do. We don't have to look at the phone or tablet, read the news in the newspaper (options especially suitable for those who have breakfast in the bar), turn on the television or radio, don't plan the day. Let us dedicate ourselves to ourselves and those dear to us who are close to us. In particular, we become aware that a new day is beginning, and that starting with us, dear reader, my day is also your day. And we can both do a lot to make an impact. Over time, the mantra: I don't know what will happen to me today it's becoming I don't know today what I'll have the chance to do. Do you understand the difference? From suffering, to acting. A real change of mentality. Almost a Copernican revolution.

Now we will dress (it goes without saying that if we had breakfast at the bar, we dressed first). Let's not do it at random, but we carefully choose clothes and above all, colors because they express something about us and above all condition our mood. An even more important thing is the vow to be kind, sincere, benevolent, altruistic. Personally, I'm not a fan of sincerity at all costs, if you risk hurting a person with it or if it can cause problems. Better silence or even better not to say what we think. We don't have to express ourselves over everything.

Before getting dressed or just leaving the house, (re) brush your teeth. I try to do it twice every morning and while we do it we pay attention not to waste too much water, just like every time we use it

So, we woke up, we got out of bed, we washed, we had breakfast and we got dressed. Nothing strange compared to the usual. Only we did it with a different approach, dedicating more time to ourselves and our loved ones. Above all, with the desire to ensure that the usual routine leaves room for a day in which we will do everything to be happy, to be serene, to realize ourselves, to make it unique and unforgettable.

A tip: let's not get up early. Rather we reflect that by doing so we will be able to take advantage of it. I, for example, slowly carbide, so the sooner I wake up, the more awake I am (cum grano salis).[27]

Sometimes, in contrast to the ritual, I drink a coffee before meditation.

To walk

Yeah, c'mon bro, I don't wanna meditate. I hate sitting cross-legged.

Ok, maybe it was a little too much, but it is true that many find excuses. Here, I will reveal something shocking to you: to meditate, you don't need to sit with your legs crossed. Indeed, it is not really necessary to sit: you can do it even while walking. The important thing is that you walk slowly, inhaling and exhaling well. In this way, the world will become almost part of you and will be more benevolent. Thanks to the inspiration the world becomes part of us, thanks to the exhalation we return it 'digested', by now familiar.

I will tell you more: not only will you notice many more details and many elements that you did not notice before, but memories will emerge related to the place where you are doing your meditative walk. The place will become so familiar to you, that after a while you will proceed like a lion in the middle of the savannah.

It doesn't matter that this happens on the seashore, in a path, or in the center of a metropolis. The important thing is that you breathe and listen to your breath. Another very important factor is that one has to walk for the sake of walking and not to reach a goal. And if we decide to meditate while we go somewhere, we need to act like we're not going anywhere.

Thanks to it, in fact, we will be able to calm the nerves and relax. If we are in a city different from ours, it is a way to make friends with it.

One of my first meditations focused on walking. Of course, we started sitting cross-legged. To tell the truth, they made us put in the most comfortable position, then they made us walk, even with our eyes closed, asking us to pay great attention to our steps. Today I try as soon as I can to do itinerant meditation and it also helps me a lot in practical activities, for example when I have a work appointment. Also, I notice the details even when I'm in a hurry, let alone when I meditate.

For Zen it is preferable that we start doing things with the left foot because the heart is on the left. But immediately after that the right one must come, that of rationality. In short, they support each other and we need both components. The movement must start from the pelvis and at the beginning we must pay attention to the legs, after a short time the rest of the body will also "start talking to us". Meditation starts from the body and then passes into our inner part. Some Zen books refer to spirit and heart, but the first word has religious implications, and as for the heart, it is known that it is somewhat overrated. Our stomach feels the emotions, not the heart. But it usually said so, and therefore we accept it. Let's keep on with the conversation, and even our walk. Breathing. What we have to do during the walk must be done calmly, and it must start only when we are well aware that we are walking.

Also in this chapter we have seen how it is possible to transform a simple daily action carried out practically by everyone into an occasion of meditation and inner growth and search for harmony with the world. In other words, in a Zen experience. Because it is true that we take four steps to relax, but with Zen there is a qualitative leap that is given by meditation and awareness.

In the kitchen

How amazing is to eat, and how also to cook (at least for me)! And how nice to eat and cook in a zen way! We have seen before that Zen leaves people free to eat what they want and if you eat chocolate brioche every morning and sometimes French fries will not be the end of the world, but it is true that it prefers a cuisine based on herbal ingredients. and fish. Above all, it prefers seasonal ingredients. Even more important is the approach to food, both in terms of preparation and consumption.

When we are preparing our meal, let's try to be in tune with food, to treat it gently, to understand how it can be cooked at the best. Some even talk to him and listen to him, a bit like the character of Maurizio Crozza[28]. It may seem a bit of an exaggeration, but it is true that an ingredient can speak to us in its own way to suggest us, based on taste, color, texture or perfume, the way of being prepared and the combinations (each dish, according to Zen, it must contain a sweet, a salty, a spicy, a bitter and an acid part, and we find this idea also in other oriental cuisines, including the Middle Eastern one). Let us remember that we eat almost exclusively what was alive and that in a sense we make it part of ourselves by ingesting it. Anaxagoras said that everything is in everything, and that it is thanks to food that hair, nails, etc. grow, as if they were already there. Freud, on the other hand, lets us know that cannibals eat their enemies to take their strength and their virtues. It is also very important that you cook with love and dedication, so that these feelings pass into food and are passed on to those who consume it. Also the choice of the products with which one prepares to eat, or with which one eats is not a matter of little importance. We try to opt for natural ones, such as wood, or glass. However, wood has the problem of being inflammable and of absorbing tastes and odors, even those of detergent, therefore it is better to rinse it thoroughly under running water. However, each element has its peculiarities and must be treated with care.[29]

When we decide what to eat, let's listen and let us not be influenced by advertising. Let's try to understand what are the foods that we really want. That maybe that desire conceals a need of our body, which uses this means to communicate it to us. Vitamins, proteins, sugars. So, let's not take our culinary desires as mere whims.

Even the moment of consumption has its own rules. As we have seen when talking about breakfast, we try to think mainly about the meal and the diners, we turn off television, radio, cell phones and other electronic devices. Eventually, we can have the meal accompanied by good background music. We should be silent, and if we are eating with someone, our meal must have priority. We should eat calmly, catching all the flavors, all the smells and all the sounds of food. The Zen meal is synesthetic. Let's try to be elegant and to use well folded cloth napkins, crystal (at least) glasses and a gratifying tableware.

There are five meditations related to food and they are

1) The elements that make up food are the same as those that make up our body. When we eat something, we are eating a part of the universe.

1) The relationship between us and food is mutual and that's why when we eat we must be present and aware

2) We need to understand what we really need and if while we're eating we are too busy talking to others or watching TV, this awareness can fail. Indeed, it will almost certainly fail.

3) Food must make us reflect on the fact that we are inextricably linked with the rest of humanity, because there have been people who cooked it and put their energy into it. Not to mention the rest of the supply chain.

4) We must be aware of the fact that what we eat will become part of our body, and for this we must honor it by using our body well, preferably doing good to others and living in harmony with them. Simply stated, if I were food, I would like to be eaten by a good person!

But we must also pay attention to the shopping phase, making it with awareness and without being conditioned by colored envelopes and offers. And when we cook, let's try to think of the most suitable recipe for our ingredients.

Even if we eat slowly, we will feel even more satisfied.

Three final considerations.

The first is that some of these councils are already becoming familiar to us For example, some cooking programs insist on combining multiple components and textures, though not like Zen. Another point on which the chefs insist is the plating and, as it happens, the presentation of the dishes is very important for Zen. However, those who practice Zen cannot appreciate certain excesses and certain freak scenes that are seen in these tv shows. Even the fact that there is a competition can't be seen with a good eye, because in a kitchen must reign harmony and not competition.

The second is that it is not very different from when in some families you decide to turn off the TV during lunch and/or dinner or when on Sunday we eat with the beautiful service. Except that for Zen we should try to do this every day.

For the third, I want to tell a personal episode. I had dinner at a kosher restaurant once. Being ignorant on the subject, I expected to find some kind of specialties, instead there were quite normal dishes, nothing shocking. Why this? Because cooking is above all a way of approaching food with an inner attitude, based on ideas or precepts. In the same way also Zen

We must understand that what we eat will transform it into energy, but also into emotions. Borges wrote that every word contains the infinite. Likewise, every bite is full of life and its energy. We should be grateful because we couldn't survive without food, and we also need to reflect that we are luckier than many other people because we can eat every day and several times a day. We must be aware of it.

The Mindfulzen [30]

The Mindfulzen is a type of meditation created by Master Carlo Tetsugen Serra.[31]

It is thought to be difficult and complicated, this because the meditator puts the mind instead of the mental presence of the heart. Meditation in the MINDFULZEN is simple and easy, if you know how to breathe you can also meditate. Meditation is conscious observation of

yourself and what you are experiencing. Meditation will not make you escape suffering, but will give you the tools to overcome it.

Meditation, especially Meditation in MINDFULZEN, concerns every moment of our life.

Every moment can be lived with awareness and through the kind observation of ourselves, every moment of life becomes unique and wonderful. Therefore meditation is our whole life when we become aware of it.

Meditation is conscious observation of yourself and what you are experiencing. Meditation will not make you escape suffering, but will give you the tools to overcome it.

There are no particular moments

There are moments to eat, others to sleep, moments suitable for social relationships, and others for solitude, and others to affirm oneself; everything can have the best time to express itself, but every moment is the right one to know yourself, so don't wait for particular moments to be aware, but start from where you are here and now MINDFULZEN.

Meditating MINDFULZEN exercises the three fundamental qualities

Concentration

It helps to keep the mind firm in what you are doing, concentration enriches you with energy because it makes you live concentrated in the here and now. Being careful means becoming aware of what you are experiencing.

Exercising attention with meditation increases the ability to process present information in real time to become aware.

Awareness

The quality of our life depends on the degree of awareness with which we live it. The result of attention is awareness, if we are attentive and have an open heart and mind, we cannot help but be aware. Awareness is the bridge between us and reality.

Mindfulzen helps us to accept reality, helps us to choose what to do, in what to commit ourselves, to develop our values, benevolence and insight. It helps us to consider thoughts for what they are, thoughts, in fact, and not objective reality, and to keep them in mind without identifying ourselves with them. It helps us to take action to improve our lives and that of others, and of the environment around us.

There are eight Mindfulzen teachings: no judgment, patience, a beginner's mind, no expectations, acceptance, letting go and love

The four conscious truths:

- Life is wonderful, but it is characterized by suffering

- The origin of suffering is attachment to the self

- The elimination of attachment to the ego makes us stop suffering

- The awakening of the conscious mind ends the suffering.

The conscious mind has these characteristics:

Mental presence, investigation and search for wisdom, joy of being on the journey, favorable energy in mind and body, mind without stress of personal attainment, concentration, equal mind.

The eight attitudes of awareness or awareness free of preconceptions, thinking based on awareness, the word based on awareness, consciously acting in reality here and now, consciously living our lives with respect for others and in harmony with them, the awareness of having a mind conditioned by the ego, consciously engaging others, having the awareness of being interdependent with others, and being aware of our commitment to the reality of our journey.

We will thus arrive to behave ethically.

Awareness is also useful to consciousness. Thanks to it, our free and positive emotions will be released, and we will be more available towards others, and towards us. We will be free from fear and selfishness, from illusions and suffering.

Beyond meditation

Whoever makes zen, who is a Buddhist or follows some principles, does not limit himself to meditating, but acts in order to make the world a better place.

Circulate your love

Among the moral actions of Zen that I like the most, there is the precept not to return the good to those who did it to us, but to do it to a third person. In this way, we will create a common good that will benefit many people. This is perfectly consistent with the Buddhist vision that sees us all bound and united by the fact of being made of the same essence, and by the fact of being transient. Therefore, let us try to do good. We are all interconnected.

Generosity and benevolence must not only concern human beings, but also other living beings. Even the plants. We are also interconnected with them.

Do you know the Zen phrase of one-handed sound? How do you interpret it? I do so: we need others, as one hand needs the other to make a sound come out.

We do good in a disinterested way, and sooner or later it will come back, says the Zen. We do not say that life is a spinning wheel, and that everything we do, whether good or bad, will be returned to us one day? And then, if not on this earth, at least we will have a reward in the Hereafter. But the Zen does not believe in the afterlife, and speaks of happiness and recognition already on this Earth. Indeed, only on this Earth, and wants happiness to be shared. For this reason there are ritual recurrences in which the sweets are offered to the Buddha and are shared with the neighbors.

To bring more happiness to the world we should learn to think big and do something useful for others. At the same time, we must not neglect small actions, both because the big actions are small actions (Scrooge McDuck docet with his Number One), and because a small action can do a lot. It can do a lot because it starts to improve the world, and because it can be taken as an example. Kant said: act as if your actions could become an example of universal b

In Milan, in Corso Buenos Aires, I saw a boy cleaning his street corner. He had a sign that said he wanted to keep that part of the world clean.

As I write this book, there is a lot of talk about a Swedish girl named Greta Thunberg, who with her perseverance moved the conscience of many of her peers.

Don't you find them both a little Zen? You too can do it.

Finally, don't you find that the use of suspended coffee is a small summary of all this?

Don't be afraid to make mistakes

An error is just a wrong approach to a question or problem. Each of them is nothing but a way to get to the right method. Indeed, for some questions we cannot even use the yes-no, true-false scheme because they are larger, and therefore need a more complex answer. In these cases, the Japanese respond with the word nu. In this case, one cannot even speak of a wrong answer.[33]

It tells of a school where students were invited to make more mistakes in order to be able to laugh about them in the future. In this way the fear of making a mistake would have been exorcised, and the mistakes would have been taken for what they are: attempts to reach the truth.[34]

Even in our culture we are quite lenient towards those who make mistakes. Just think of the proverbs "Error is only human" (which, however, is completed by the part that reads " but to persist in it, is diabolical!") and "Practice makes perfect". However, an ancient Greek motto reads: en pathei, mazon. In suffering, learning. The path to knowledge is not easy.

Dancing leaves

In Zen monasteries everything is regulated, and the monks know well in advance what they will have to do at a given time. They claim to be free only in this way, because they are no longer slaves of the moment and its contingency. I don't know, everyone adjusts as he believes.

I think a little bit about myself

When you are aware of reality and of yourself, deep love will be born within you for everything and for everyone, for all our beauty, as well as for all our imperfections. The compassionate state is born, a loving acceptance of everything. Love for yourself will turn into love towards every moment of life, and envelops everything you do, including people.[35]

Doing meditation, eating well, having fulfilling sex, having a garden, walking in Zen mode, are all ways to feel good. I want to add two.

We must gratify ourselves, and notice when we get success, when we do something positive. Some tend not to give weight to the good things they do, or to pass them over in silence. Instead, satisfaction frees dopamine, and dopamine stimulates the urge to do.

We must also forgive ourselves. Did we cheat, did we make a mistake? Be patience, we will fix that.

It seems to me that the meaning is quite clear: we must try to feel good, because that's what we strive to with others.

Also for our culture forgiveness (the forgiveness of sins) and the recognition of value are important, but we want them to come from third parties. Just blend in, says a proverb. Instead, Zen teaches us that we can be aware of our success and our value, without being snooty or old geezers.

Even those who absolve themselves, are not seen very well. Zen teaches us to forgive ourselves.

A little healthy selfishness helps altruism.

Our joy can shine in favor of others.

Seeing what hurts others can make us think about what is or is not necessary. After all, hasn't Buddhism started like this?

The teachings serve us just to understand the necessary things and the things that can also be done without.

Paradoxically, Zen tells us that if we conquer the firmness of the mind we can afford not to completely detach ourselves from earthly things.

Another paradox: the desire not to have attachments to earthly pleasures risks becoming an attachment in itself. Zen does not want us to become moralists or ascetics.

Take advantage of what we don't like about us

Let's go over this one more time: the Zen states that we must accept the things that we don't like. Here, however, we are taking a shot: we must try to make it a strong point. Like the nun who painted with her mouth.

Another nun (the first American Buddhist nun) wrote that we must feed our demons to draw strength from them.[36]

Garrincha, a Brazilian player, had one leg shorter than the other and the lameness made it easier to dribble through opponents. Too bad that not everyone knows how to dribble, or play in the Brazilian national team.

Maybe we get a little closer to this Zen idea with resilience. Sometimes there is also awareness.

Examples of closeness between
the two cultures

Are Western and Zen culture really that far? The word creates the world, and throughout the book I will give you examples that can show you that many of the things we do, or that are part of our Western culture, already have something of Zen in them and could make our journey easier. But we lack the awareness of it, and someone to help us do it. Only then can we say: "I am doing something applying the principles of Zen".

There is a writer who can represent a trait-d-union between the West and Japan, and she is the Belgian Amelie Nothomb. The daughter of a diplomat, she was born and raised in Japan, even though she left her native country when she was a child and followed her father in China and other Far Eastern countries. The latter makes some mention in a book called "Biography of Hunger" and elsewhere, but Japan, one of its rockstar literary production (really prolific) and Nothomb makes us know many aspects, even grotesque and paradoxical. In fact, I discovered aspects of Japan that I didn't really know by reading Nothomb's books. I would like to focus on one step. In "Metaphysics of the tubes", she, an unmanageable child, is calmed by a piece of Belgian white chocolate.[37]

Have you seen Kill Bill, Quentin Tarantino's eastern western? Do you remember the scene in which the Bride

(Uma Thurman, for instance), wakes up after a very long coma? What moves first thing? The feet. This has a very Zen meaning, and we must not exclude that the reference is wanted, given the director's interest in that culture.

Drieu La Rochelle[38] he was a French writer who went down in history because he was a Nazi, a Stalinist, a collaborator and a suicide seeker. He wanted to annihilate his own self to merge with the universal whole. Although not very edifying, it is another example of closeness between the West and the East. Isn't one of the principles of Buddhism Nirvana, that is, the place where all subjectivity is lost?

Anyone who has studied a bit of philosophy knows that much importance is given to the senses as data collectors that the mind then reworks, and also knows that our mind shapes the shape of the world. Man is the measure of all things, is a principle of Renaissance philosophy, and finds its analogue in one of Zen.

He also knows in the early days that he sought the first principle, the element of which all beings are constituted. Thales hypothesized that it was water.

Excluding for reasons diametrically opposed Thales and the Nothomb, we do not know if the cases we have seen above derive from a knowledge of oriental culture, or anyway of an influence, or if they are simply the result of a coincidence (another principle dear to Zen) and, ultimately, we don't even care. What interested us was the fact that we are not so far away, and we will return in the course of the book. We understand that some things we do are already zen, only that we need to work on it.

Zen, Network and the world

We mentioned before the vegan cook imitated by Maurizio Crozza. Now let's talk about another character from the Genoese comedian, Napalm 51. Who is Napalm 51? Napalm 51 represents the haters. The haters, the word itself says it, but surely you will already know it, they are people who vent their anger on the Internet, especially on social networks. We leave out the question of fake news because it goes beyond this context, even if the two concepts are often linked, and let's focus on anger. If Napalm 51 began to listen to their own feelings, even the negative ones, they would be able to understand and accept them, finding a more peaceful way of expressing and controlling them. Because we all have moments of anger, and anger must not be repressed, but we must only not let it turn into rage.

The main point is that for Zen every man is enlightened, only that all those obstacles that prevent the light from radiating must be eliminated. Zen and practices help us do it. In this way, the hater character created by Crozza would stop insulting, and even click and share compulsively. The abuse of the Internet that many do is a form of greed 2.0. Also for this reason the Zen advises to switch off the mobile devices from time to time, at least during meals. It absolutely does not ask to live without, because it has fallen into the world and is indeed a way to live better within it. Why, let it be known, "The Buddha, the Divine, dwells in the circuit of a computer or in the gears of the change of a motorcycle with the same ease as atop a mountain or in the petals of a flower". [39]

Zen does not even want us to renounce pleasure and gratification, or that we punish ourselves in penance. It simply tells us that we must seek the source of happiness within us, so that it is more stable and more lasting. Events outside of us can change, indeed they will almost certainly change and some will be painful. If we entrust our happiness exclusively to the outside world, when things go wrong, how will we do it? On the contrary, the happiness that comes from within will not be subject to so many changes. Let's take it as a useful tip. But do you advise us to be insensitive to the pain of others or not to feel them? Absolutely not. Pain exists, it must be accepted and Zen helps us do it.

Of course, superficial things can give us pleasure, and pleasure should not be rejected, but we will find true happiness by coming into harmony with our deepest part.

Jung spoke of me and The Self, and for him dreams are the bridge between the two components of our personality, while for Zen it is meditation.

Answer to the objections of the previous chapter

Someone will dispute: but if we already have these habits, why bring up Zen? I refer above all to that of counting up to ten. Because there is a difference, which is that we understand that Zen has negative feelings, and we accept them. We say that it is as if there were a sort of splitting thanks to which we perceive our negative part (or obscure, as some claim). We are aware of this. In general, some uses that we have in the West or that we are adopting in the West are bricks that help us build our Zen home, but we must also put other types of bricks and, what matters most, the house will be special. In short, it is not enough to put chopsticks to be a Japanese restaurant. We must also pay attention to the elements that we have and which they lack, and also to understand that in some cases it is a structural non-presence. I refer to the almost total absence of speculation, as we have already seen. A bit like a fat-free kitchen. Amelie Nohthomb said that Japanese monuments are built and designed to be admired in the dark.[40]. One more case in which the absence of something, in this case the light of the sun, becomes structural.

The second objection is that there are ways to channel anger, such as sport and artistic sublimation. Well, those who already succeed in these ways, probably don't need Zen. The point is that Zen is not only useful for managing anger and aggression.

A bit of pop

Zen and sex

Zen is not bigot. It does not condemn homosexuality and neither does sex only for pleasure. He recognizes it as an integral part of life, and invites only to do it with awareness and respect for other people. He does not condemn even those who resort to prostitution, or those who resort to masturbation. Above all with regard to the latter, he knows that it is a natural thing and asks only that it be done in a balanced way, avoiding disorders, excesses and upsets. What is the limit? Everyone must understand their own.

Moreover, it could not be otherwise: not having a metaphysical basis and, above all, not having a transcendent idea, it certainly cannot have a rigid moral doctrine in certain fields of self related to subjectivity and individual choices such as food and sexuality. Let's say that Zen gives us advice on how to live better, not precepts.

Zen, and in general all Buddhism, in the sexual sphere leaves to the laity freedom. He only asks that one not deal with people who are engaged or married, with mental patients and with prisoners or ex-prisoners. He also asks, and that is what matters most, that people and their happiness are placed at the center of everything, therefore also of the sexual sphere. I do not agree with the ban on having sex with former prisoners, given that once a sentence has been served a person regains the right to a normal life, without talking about the consequences. As you can see, I have a detached approach to this practice and this religion.

This time I will not write conclusions to the chapter by making parallels between Western and Zen behavior, but I add a note of color: Jennifer Aniston [41] is a fan of Zen sex.

I want to add a sort of quote instead. Have you seen the movie Sex and Zen? I did, and found it quite grotesque, but in retrospect it was simply ironic. Irony as a detachment, which is one of the cornerstones of Buddhism. We also find a desire to overcome and learn, but learn in a practical way, for concrete things, in full Zen style.[42]

A Buddhist sutra states: do not waste love and sex, and literature on Zen and sex is not lacking.

Another Buddhist thought holds that passions are a road to enlightenment.

Osho[43] ha wrote a book entitled "Secrets and mysteries of eros"[44]. It seems to me that space is given to this human component, and without condemnations or morbidity. What do you think about it?

The Zen gardens

In an episode of the cartoon, the Simpsons set up a Zen garden. This is my first memory of these Japanese wonders, in which one goes to meditate, and which do not have an aesthetic function. The elements and their arrangement constitute a fundamental part of it. Great importance is given to water, to which zen itself attaches great importance.

The Japanese name with which the Zen gardens are indicated is Karesansui, which means *"stone gardens"*. Its origins date back to Japanese Shintoism. Buddhist monks have taken over Japanese gardens to have a space within the monasteries where they can meditate and pray better. But it is possible can create this corner of peace in which to reflect even in non-religious places..[45] From a religious point of view, the Japanese garden is **naturocentric** (unlike the Western one, which is defined as anthropocentric), **asymmetrical** and **apparently random**; expresses the harmony of man with nature. Each element corresponds to something. The sand symbolizes water and the stones symbolize the islands. We have to make drawings on the sand that imitate the waves. The stones must always be odd, and above all never four, because the Japanese associate it with death. [46] It is preferable that a Zen garden is small and fenced. Care must be taken constantly, but doing it is not difficult because they are "dry gardens", which need little water.[47]

In this way we can enter the discourse of Zen minimalist architecture, and think that even our architecture, and above all our design are becoming very minimalist [48]. Let's also consider local buildings like the Bosco Verticale in Milan.

Can't you see a Zen influence here too?

The carps

Those of you who have ever played Pokémon Go, played with cards, or have seen the cartoon, will surely remember Magikarp. What is it? It is a very weak fish that evolves into Gyarados, a dragon that is also one of the most fearsome Pokémon. according to legend there is a waterfall and the carps that go beyond it become dragons. In fact, the creators were inspired by this legend. What does it mean? It means that everyone has the chance to make a qualitative leap, and to become an enlightened person. Indeed, to return to it.

This does not seem sacrilegious: the Japanese are used to using cartoons to spread the culture, and to make children approach you too. Think for example of Lady Oscar and Pollon.

Even the Buddhist deities choose unusual and unexpected ways to reach their goal. Bodhisattva Kuan Yin, who represents the feminine energy ofcompassion took the form of a seductive fisherwoman and promised to marry those who had learned some sutras. After a while he died, and he made his husband promise to remember her by spreading the teaching of the Buddha.[49]

Some interesting facts [50]

When they enter the convent the monks make an offer for their own funeral.

The Buddhist temple is called sangha.

In Japanese, the prolonged retreats in which one meditates are called sesshin, which translates as a "union of minds", while in Korean the expression is "yong meng Jong non", meaning "when you're sitting, jump like a tiger". The newly appointed monk is called a shukke, a homeless monk.

The monks vow to follow the eight teachings of the Buddha (also called The Eightfold Path). Eight meditations that must be learned with the heart, and put into practice. They are right view, right resolve, right speech, right livelihood, right effort, right mindfulness, and right samadhi ('meditative absorption or union').

The silence is very important thanks to which we will enter into harmony with the deepest part of us, and will awaken compassion, empathy, tenderness and love. They promote happiness.

Tenzo is the monk who takes care of the kitchen. He wakes up before the others to eat, and goes to bed last after fixing everything. Our culture considers those who serve others to be of lower rank, whereas in the Zen monasteries the tenzo is second only to the prior of the convent in hierarchy.

More questions

Are there Zen monasteries in Italy?

Yes, there are eight. One in Milan, one in Berceto (Pr), one in Brescia, one in Cantù (Co), one in Cecina (Li), one in Padua, one in Naples and one in Avellino. Some are open to the laity, who can go and spend a few days to experience the zen with the monks.

What do we owe to Zen?

The haiku poetic form, the tea ceremony, the art of arranging flowers (ikebana), the art of calligraphy (shodō), painting (zen-ga), Japanese theater (Nō), culinary art (zen-ryōri, shojin ryōri, fucharyōri), martial arts such as aikido, judo and karate, the art of the sword (kendō) and archery (kyūdō)[51]. But also in the kitchen field, with zen-ryori, shojin-ryori and fucha-ryori. If you think about it, the dishes we eat at the Japanese restaurant are made with the ingredients we've seen to be the basis of Zen food, and we're not just referring to food.[52]

Where is the oldest Zen temple in the world?

The oldest Zen temple in the world is Tofuku-ji and is located in Kyoto and dates back to the 12th century.

When did Zen spread in the West?

It is difficult to say, but certainly an important period is the end of the 19th century. It is certain that the first official conversion was that wife of Alexander Russel in 1906. A very important role was given by Daisets Teitaro Suzuki (1869-1955), with her books, of which we remember the Essays in Zen Buddhism.[53]

The Zenroma website reports instead:

Spread over the centuries from India to China to Japan, and then throughout Asia, it arrived in Europe, France, through Master Taisen Deshimaru in 1967 and is now practiced and known throughout the world.[54]

Do Zen nuns exist?

Yes of course.

Experiences, stories and anecdotes

Welcome to the most creative part of the book, where you will find some personal inspiration.

Zen, football and archery

Andrea played football, and dreamed of making a memorable goal, but no matter how hard he tried, though he resigned himself to crossing the posts, despite having a correct body posture, and trying to calibrate the shot well. He didn't have square feet, yet he couldn't. Even one would have been enough, even if people said it was the "best Sunday goal", which was just luck.

He changed many coaches, but with all he had the same result. He was good, but he was thinking of quitting.

Then one day he came across a Japanese. Yes it was a Zen football master, who told him "You have to understand that you don't have to aim for the seven, and you don't have to think about how you put the body or what part of the foot you hit the ball. You just have to learn to breathe well, that's the key to everything. "

Andrea tried it out in a game: he breathed the way the Japanese master had taught him, kicked the ballwithout thinking too much, and a masterpiece came out of it.

It was not only thanks to the technique that he succeeded, but above all to the fact of not having thought of the gesture, of having done it by creating the void, and merging consciousness and unconscious. He had outgrown the technique, and the technique had become an inapprehensive art, gushed from the unconscious.[55]

Andrea made that great goal by performing a Zen action. What do you mean? In the sense that he did it in a natural way without thinking too much on how to do that.

The Japanese are not very good at playing football, on the other hand they are good at shooting with a bow, and they know that you become skilled archers, only when the mind stops focusing on the details of what it is doing. Only in this way, the technique learned will come out.

And it can come out because it has become introjected, it has become ours, indeed, it has become a part of us.

The Japanese are not very good at playing soccer (although they have improved a lot lately), but years ago they created a cartoon in "Japan wins the world championship"[56]. Yes it is Holly and Benji, as many of you have guessed. Well, the champion Holly often said this sentence: "The ball is your friend". Because with friends we can be natural and do things without thinking about it, naturally. And those with friends are moments when we are free, and we offer the best part of us. But the ball does not become everyone's friend and above all it does not become a friend immediately, except in very rare cases. We need to become familiar with it. In this respect it is not very dissimilar from the Japanese bow, which is not immediately given immediately, but requires so much exercise. They are similar also for another fact: just as a good shooter with an average value bow shoots an arrow better than a mediocre shooter with a higher bow, in the same way a good footballer will do more dribbles with a normal ball, than a poor one with a latest-generation ball. Above all, the two good ones will almost certainly do it thinking less than the less gifted ones.[57]

What interests us is the naturalness that is achieved only when we are completely detached from ourselves, and that it is one with the perfection of technical ability. It is when things come to us very well, not "though we don't think" but "because we don't think about it".

In one passage of the book 'Zen and archery', the master strikes in a room lit only by a very dim light, first the target, and then with a second arrow, the first arrow. It hits them from a very respectable distance. It is not only a question of technique, but also of introjected technique, which allows you to pull as you pull. In another part of the book, the master gets angry with the protagonist, because he uses a shortcut based only on technique, concentrating excessively on what he is doing.

Zen focuses on a gesture: breathing. Breathing that moves our inner life. We a little less.[58]

Painters and zen

I once spoke with a Milanese artist. He marveled at the many meanings I managed to find in his works. He told me that the images went directly from the unconscious to his hand. Of course I don't know how to paint, so I look for hidden meanings in artistic works. In addition he, like almost all artists, was concrete, not speculative, lived his own art and in this sense was more zen than the best. Best: it was potentially, in the philosophical meaning of power, more zen than me.

Have you ever talked to an artist, especially a painter? It can be very disappointing, especially if one had the illusion of learning some hidden meaning of the picture, in particular details, some elements or chromatic choices. Often they are of a disarming simplicity, and all this can be twice Zen. First of all, because it teaches us the value of self-practice. The painter paints the picture because he likes that image or idea, or because he was commissioned. It has an overview of the picture, then the details come later, you will think about it. Although the most delicious aspects of the works are often linked to the details. From Caravaggio who used prostitutes as models for sacred figures, to Luini who gave a woman who was about to be delivered the face of an ex-lover, from the Judas of Leonardo who would have the appearance of the prior, to the many anonymous girls who , as Sebastiano Vassalli informs us, just as anonymous madonnas did pose to paint precisely the Madonna. End of the digression, let's get back to us and our Zen. Disarming artists can be on the zen path for another reason. Because they don't think, they don't think speculatively and rationally, but they think, like the rain that falls. According to a way of saying, those who can't do, teach. Here, painters know how to do, so they don't teach. And whoever does not even know how to teach is a critic and finds senses that have even escaped the author himself. He had the key element, which is naturalness. Because he had introjected his art.

A few years ago I followed a tai-chi lesson. While I practiced some positions, I reflected on the fact that they are not so different from movements that we can do in our gym or at home doing some physical activity. The same happened to me with the position of the warrior during stretching. But there were more elements. The first is poetry, which we miss a little. There is a difference between doing a lunge and making the position of a warrior. The second. it is concentration on what you are doing. Not that we miss you, but I perceived it differently there. We focus on repetitions, loads, posture, recovery time. In tai-chi, I perceived attention to the gesture in its entirety, and it was so beautiful that you hardly noticed that you were doing things you can do even in the gym. Have you ever seen children play empty sack full bag? They enjoy carefree, but they are doing squats.

Who is an expert on Zen, would say that we are faced with examples of Satori, in which the differences between subject and object, and between conscience and unconscious cancel each other out. It is not an immediate thing. Therefore, here is a more appropriate explanation to us;

Zen culture is closely linked to gesture, to repetition as perfection, to the moment when thought is nullified, and only action counts. It is a philosophy that is applied in many disciplines related to Japanese culture, in which the hand that draws a mark with the brush can be the same as holding a kendo sword. **There is no hesitation within a pure Zen gesture,** because that gesture has become so much a part of you, that your body executes it without the mind being involved. **It is the muscle memory of the athlete who does not think, but acts.** Yoda's motto of Star Wars, which not by chance incorporates within itself the appearance, ways and many of the philosophies of a Zen master, was **"Do or Do not, there is no Try".**[59]

In Summary

Zen Buddhism (or better, Dharma, as it is known in the East) is a Japanese school that came to Japan thanks to the expansion of the Mahayana doctrine (great vehicle), or an anti-substantialistic and anti metaphysical philosophy (birth and death are Nirvana, illusions are illumination) which denies dualism. Zen is a monastic tradition based on the lineage (transmission of dharma from master to disciple), martial and very Japanese, made of rituals sometimes a bit complicated, anti-intellectual, and with a taste for paradox (koans). Essential and practical discipline, it has produced the aesthetics that we recognize as peculiar to Japan (the gardens, the minimal and very illuminated spaces).

The fundamental formal practice is zazen, or sitting meditation. Other practices are walking meditation, and particular rituals that mark the fundamental stages of the journey, or discipline (dharma or dhamma in pali means discipline, rule, law and many other things). Attention to food, from preparation to presentation, conviviality, and no room for intellectual speculation.

The lineage is what is transmitted from master to disciple, and this happens not through words but through observation.

The Buddhist Zen doctrine is founded like the same Chán Buddhism from which it strictly derives, on the refusal to recognize authority to the Buddhist scriptures (*sutra*[60]).

This does not mean that Zen rejects the Buddhist scriptures. Indeed, some of them, such as the *Heart Sutra*, the *Vimalakīrti Nirdeśa Sūtra* or the same *Laṅkāvatārasūtra*.

Zen avoids intellectual speculation, and is also distinguished from other Mahāyāna Buddhist schools for having centralized the meditative practice (*zazen*) in its *shikantaza* forms (meditation on breath, mind and emptiness, performed by sitting) or accompanied by study of the *kōan*.

Appendix

Examples of Koan

A monk asked Chao-chou: "I entered this monastery right now. I ask the patriarch to explain the doctrine to me ».

Chao-chou replied, "Have you already eaten your boiled rice?"

The monk said, "I've already eaten it."

Chao-chou said, "Then go and wash the bowl."

The monk was enlightened.

To see clearly our image, we just need to clean the mirror

**

If you can't do anything, what can you do?

***

The master asked, "Who is hindering you?" The student: "Nobody hinders me". The master replied: "So, what need is there to seek liberation?"

***

A monk asked Chao-Chou: "If a poor man comes, what should he be given?" "He lacks nothing," replied the master.

***

If we move the boulders, the river will also change its course.

***

You can bring the thirsty ox to the river, but if he does not drink, he will die.
***

The fundamental illusion of humanity is to assume that I am here, and you are there.
***

We meditate on what we really want. Ave

Appendix 2

"The purpose of the Zen" (D. T. Suzuki)

Let's read for the last time some excerpts from the first volume of Essays on Zen Buddhism by D.T. Suzuki:

"The state in which every remnant of conceptual consciousness has vanished is called a state of poverty by Christian mystics. The definition of Tauler is: "Absolute poverty is in you, when you do not know how to remember if someone owes you something, or if you owe something to someone: just as everything will be forgotten by you, in the final journey of death".

[...] Wu-men (Mumon) sings:

Ten thousand flowers in spring, the moon in autumn,

a cool breeze in summer, snow in winter.

If your mind isn't clouded by unnecessary things,

this is the best season of your life.

Here other verses, by Shou-an (Shuan):

At Nantai I sit quietly with an incense burning,

One day of rapture, all things are forgotten,

Not that mind is stopped and thoughts are put away,

But that there is really nothing to disturb my serenity.

[...]The disciple of Zen [...] can be fully active [...] - and yet his spirit is filled with a happiness and a transcendent calm. [...] All the desires have fallen from his heart, no vain thought obstructs the flow of vital activity, and so he is empty and "poor". In his poverty he knows how to enjoy "spring flowers" and "autumnal moon". Until worldly riches were accumulated in his heart, there was no place for this transfigured joy. [...]

The purpose of Zen is to achieve what is technically called the "non-acquisition" state. All knowledge is acquisition and accumulation, while Zen aims to free us from all possession. The spirit must make us poor and humble, completely free of inner impurities. Instead, knowledge is rich and arrogant. [...]Zen certainly adheres to what Lao-tze says (*Tao-te-ching*, XLVIII): « Those who seek knowledge are enriched day by day. The one who seeks the Tao becomes poor from day to day. It becomes increasingly poor as long as it reaches non-action (*wu-wei*). With non-acting, there is nothing he cannot reach». In its perfection, this kind of loss is the "non-acquisition", identical to poverty. In poverty, one can see a synonym of "emptiness", of *sunyata*. When the spirit has purged itself of all the waste accumulated since time immemorial, the clothes fall, the trappings fall, only a naked essence remains. Now empty, free, authentic, the spirit assumes its innate dignity. And in this there is also joy, but not the joy that can give rise to its opposite, to sadness, but an absolute joy […].

In Christianity, we think too much about God, although it is said that in him we live, we move and we have our being. Zen also wants the last trace of a dualistic consciousness of God to be erased. For this reason, it urges its followers not to stop even where the Buddha is and to pass quickly where there is no longer any Buddha " (dal cap. VII, par. XI). (http://www.lameditazionecomevia.it/suzuki14.htm)

Appendix 3

I will end with a story taken from 101 Zen Stories (https://www.visioneolistica.it/contadino-saggio-storie-zen/).

Meanwhile, read it, then I'll explain.
Here is the story of the wise peasant.

Once upon a time in a Chinese village there was an old farmer who lived with his son and a horse, which was their only source of income.

One day, the horse escaped leaving the man without the possibility of working the land.

His neighbors came to him to show them their solidarity and said they felt sorry for the incident.

He thanked them for the visit, but asked them: "How do you know if what happened to me is good or bad for me? Who knows!"

The neighbors, perplexed by the old farmer's attitude, went away.

A week later the horse returned to the stable, accompanied by a large herd of horses. When the news reached the villagers, they returned to the farmer's house, congratulating him on his good fortune.

"Before you had only one horse, and now you have many. It is a great wealth. What luck! "They said.

"Thanks for the visit and for your solidarity," he replied, but how do you know that this is good or bad for me? " The neighbors were once again baffled by the old farmer's response, and left.

Some time later, the farmer's son, in an attempt to tame one of the new horses, fell off and broke his leg.

The attentive neighbors returned to visit the farmer, proving to be very sorry for the misfortune.

The man thanked for the visit and affection of all, and again asked: "How can you know if the incident is a disgrace? Let's wait and see what happens over time. " Once again, the old farmer's phrase left everyone stunned, and without words, they left in disbelief.

A few months passed, and Japan declared war on China. The government sent its emissaries throughout the country in search of healthy young men to send to the front in battle. They arrived at the village and recruited all the young men, except the farmer's son who had a broken leg.
None of the boys came back alive. The farmer's son instead recovered, and the horses were sold with a good income.

The wise farmer went to visit his neighbors to console and help them, as they had shown solidarity with him in every situation.

Whenever some of them complained, the wise farmer said, "How do you know if this is bad?" If someone rejoiced too much, he asked him: "How do you know if this is good?"

It was at that moment that the men of the village understood the teaching of the wise farmer who urged them not to get excited and **not let themselves be overwhelmed by events, always accepting what is**, aware of the fact that, <u>beyond good and evil</u>, **everything it may be different from what it looks like**.

First of all, I decided to add this story because I read it in the book "Siamo tutti latinisti" by Cesare Marchi. I didn't know it was a Zen story, but the mixture of West and East was one of the main themes of this book. Secondly, because as a writer I always have to deal with texts. Finally, because even writing (not in the sense of calligraphy) can be zen.

Our mind can and must be full of ideas, doubts and uncertainties, before and after writing. But when you start writing, all of this disappears and becomes immediate action. For us, the artist, the genius, is what creates a unique piece, the concept of absolute originality compared to previous works and the same rules of gender, is a contemporary concept, born with romanticism. Classical art was largely serial, and the historical avant-gardes have challenged in different ways the romantic idea of creation as an absolute debut.

Repetition is essential for Zen philosophy, as it is the only way to reach perfection. The way of Zen is a journey made of patience, perseverance and self-criticism. A journey that may seem far from a varied and creative activity such as writing, but it is not necessarily the case. What in Zen remains unchanged is the gesture and the execution. Everything else changes, and we can adapt to change, only if we are totally in control of ourselves.

Before and after writing, our mind can and must be full of ideas, doubts, uncertainties, these are the main ingredients that allow our creativity. However, when we place our hands on the keyboard or pick up a pen, all of this shall disappear to become an often unconscious flow. That is the secret and beautiful alchemy that drives people to tell you "where do you get your ideas?"

It is a thought that is linked in part to what we have already seen regarding creativity. Writing must be an almost monastic exercise, a ritual made up of repetitions in which we slowly prepare our brains to step aside to make room for that part of us that allows us to bring out the concept we want to express without having to think about it. He is there, we just have to reach him and express it through writing.

There will be enough time to correct that sentence we don't like or to delete that concept, but the heart of what we write is there, and we have already found it. This is fundamental, especially in these times when the work of writing on the internet often requires very short execution times, articles that must be precise, concise and well written right away. It also binds to the idea of a workout that lasts for years, but that bears fruit just when it's needed. A perfect and totally natural execution that hides years and years of mistakes and preparation. Because luck exists, but it cannot be the only port to which a writer must refer. Luck is often just a synonym of preparation. For that moment when the train has passed, and you had your suitcase ready after training for years and years to prepare it perfectly.[61]

---

[1] A Zen master who died in 788- Cf.. Daisetz T. Suzuki, "Introduzione" to Eugen Herrigel, "Lo Zen e il tiro con l'arco", Adelphi, Milano, 1975, p.12.

[2] Fabrizio De Andrè, "Verranno a chiederti del nostro amore" (Fabrizio De Andrè-Nicola Piovani-Giuseppe Bentivoglio).

[3] American writer of German and Swedish origins born in 1928.

[4] Robert M. Pirsig, "Lo Zen e l'arte della manutenzione della motocicletta", Adelphi, Milano, 1981, p.395.

[5] http://www.treccani.it/enciclopedia/zen/

[6] http://www.zenroma.it/zen/

[7] Bodhidharma, whose life and work are located between the 5th and the 6th century AD, is one of the most indecipherable characters. The legends about him are as numerous as the verifiable historical sources are scarce. Among the few reliable data is its origin: he came from a noble family of South India. Another certain fact is his lineage, that of the XXVIII Patriarch of Buddhism, therefore a direct descendant of Siddharta Gautama (http://www.casamushin.it/bodhidharma.html)

[8] http://www.monasterozen.it/monastero-zen-il-cerchio/cosa-e-lo-zen/

[9] https://www.laciviltacattolica.it/articolo/esercizio-zen-e-meditazione-cristiana/

[10] By slightly modifying the phrase of the Viscount Cobram, the total director of Fantozzi, a fanatic of cycling, we can say that Zen is a healthy activity for everyone and from which everyone can benefit. If instead you prefer a more courtly quote, here's what Suzuki writes (see note 1) "The characteristic diversity between Zen and all other religious, philosophical or mystical doctrines, is the fact that Zen never leaves our daily life, and that, despite all the range of its practical applications of its concreteness, it has something in itself that places it outside the contamination and tumult of the theater of the world.

[11] A koan states: "Before the awakening I cut wood and carried water;
after waking up I cut wood and carried water. "We'll see what the koans are next.

[12]

http://www.gianfrancobertagni.it/materiali/zen/buddismozen.htm

[13] Nansen Osho, "Lezioni del Buddha per raggungere la serenità in 3 mesi. 90 esercizi per rendere meravigliosa la vita di tutti i giorni". Antonio Vallardi Editore, Milano, 2015, p.215.

[14] https://www.ipermind.com/filosofia-zen/

[15] I don't specify because in reality the phrase has been attributed to several people.

[16] Nan-in, a Japanese master of the Meiji era (1868-1912), received a visit from a university professor who had come to him to question him about Zen.
Nan-in served tea. He filled his guest's cup, and then continued to pour.
The professor watched as the tea spilled over, then he could no longer contain himself. «It is full. It no longer has anything to do with it! "
"Like this cup," said Nan-in, "you are filled with your opinions and conjectures. How can I explain Zen to you if you don't empty your cup first?
".(https://buddhismoitalia.forumcommunity.net/?t=55499193)

[17] In the book by Amélie Nothomb "Neither of Eve nor of Adam" there is a passage in which we talk about the fact that even in schools pupils are not used to asking questions. Instead she, who is European, asks them and it creates discomfort and embarrassment.

[18] The importance of this simple and natural gesture crosses cultures. Consider the Greek "pneuma", which indicates the breath and the vital breath, or the fact that God breathes into Adam, and he comes to life.

[19] Nansen Osho, op. cit. , pp. 212-3.

[20] Zazen means sitting meditation. To practice zazen you don't need any particular physical requirements, zazen is within everyone's reach and basically its essence lies in the fact of being "simply sitting" in a posture that facilitates concentration from which greater self-awareness is derived. During the meditation one remains seated and in silence, concentrating on breathing, on the natural coming and going of the breath, only observing it. In the same way one observes the rising and passing of thoughts, and without attachment one lets them go. Even if for many meditation is something strange, transcendent, incomprehensible, in reality it belongs to each of us, from the beginning and it is only a different way of making our body-spirit work. Beyond its spiritual and philosophical connotations, Zen is by now learned and used as a benevolent support to manage anxiety, stress and all those coercion mechanisms that make life today so difficult. Today, more than ever, techniques like Mindfulness, body relaxation, Yoga and other forms of support and development of awareness are increasingly used to free man from the burden of everyday life.

[21] https://www.meditazionezen.it/cose-la-meditazione-zen-2/

[22] A koan is literally, the transcription of a "public case" that happened in the past; or, as a Zen master said, "the place where truth is found". Generally speaking, koans are taken from authentic dialogues between Zen masters and students, or between advanced practitioners, or from sutras or ancient sayings. Most of the time, koans are paradoxical in nature, and cannot be

understood by the intellect. Thus, a koan can only be understood thanks to the direct experience of the authentic mind from which it was born. The sayings and dialogues that turned into koans are collected in various texts, such as the Mumonkan. Some scholars assert that in the early days many people chose the practice of koan to learn to cope with the sufferings of their lives. The koanoffers the opportunity for a solid practice, not only while sitting in zazen, but also in the midst of the turmoil of life. It provides the concrete means to break the bond of suffering in times of conflict and uncertainty.
(http://www.fiorediloto.org/koan.htm)

[23] Wikipedia simply translates it into just sitting

[24] The word Zazen Shikantaza: "simply sitting" means that we sit in zazen with simplicity, without goals and expectations. The secret and the difficulty lie precisely in this word: simply. When we sit in zazen, in fact, we abandon knowledge and knowledge and enter naked into the practice of being.
Shikantaza, that is to witness the reality of one's being. In Zen it is said, in fact, "Enter in Zazen, and you do not go out any more": it means that when you sit in meditation, you do it with your baggage of illusions and conditionings, thoughts and expectations, then your illusion of being a small separate me vanishes, and here is no one sitting in Zazen anymore, you are no longer as you thought before, but a universal being as you are now.

[25] https://martaalbe.com/2017/03/29/meditazione-sassolini/

[26] The meditation and breathing practices described in this book, including the shikantaza and the koan described above, are taken by Master Tetsugen Serra, "Zen 3.0, Cairo Editore, Milano, 2015, passim. Unless otherwise indicated.

[27] Cf. Nansen Osho, op. cit.

[28] Germidi Soia.

[29] For materials, cf Simone Martinelli, Zenstation, Piacere in tutti i sensi, Lit Srl-Ultra Edition, Roma, 2015, pp.57-68.

[30] http://mindfulzen.it/la-meditazione-mindfulzen/

[31] Milano, 1953-vivente. Cf. op. cit. Being the creator of the Mindfulzen, the part inherent to this discipline is taken from the parts of his book in which he speaks about it.

[32] Cf. Nansen Osho, op. cit. The next five chapters have this book as a main reference.

[33] Zen is said in the book, and the art of motorcycle maintenance.

[34] Osho reports it in the cited book.

[35] http://mindfulzen.it/la-meditazione-mindfulzen/

[36] Tsultrim Allione, "Nutri i tuoi demoni. Risolvere i conflitti interiori con la saggezza del Buddha". Oscar Mondadori, Milano, 2009.

[37] I wanted to understand chocolate as a gift from the world to the child to repair the fracture that had been created, to tell her that she wanted to welcome it. A sort of primordial element.

[38] Cf. Drieu La Rochelle, Racconto Segreto-Diario 1944-45 SE Editore, 2005.

[39] Robert M. Pircing, op. cit.

[40] In "Happy nostalgia".

[41] http://www.oggi.it/people/vip-e-star/2011/08/10/jennifer-aniston-il-sesso-zen-e-un-traguardo-importante/

[42] https://it.wikipedia.org/wiki/Sex_and_Zen_-_Il_tappeto_da_preghiera_di_carne

[43] Not the one mentioned above, but the best-known Osho, also famous for the fake phrases that run on the Net. This Osho was born in 1931 and died in 1980 and was Indian, the former is Japanese and is alive. Moreover, as regards the latter, on the second "o" there is a sign, similar to that of long vowels, which I couldn't sign.

[44] Universale Economica Feltrinelli, Milano, 2015. Pagg. 80.

[45] But it is also true that for Zen every place can be a place to meditate, and every situation can be a starting point for reflection on life and the true importance of material goods.

[46]

https://luomodimezzanotte.wordpress.com/2015/03/14/tetrafobia-la-paura-del-numero-4/

[47] Cf. https://www.ilgiardinodeilibri.it/speciali/il-giardino-zen-giardinaggio-religione-filosofia.php

[48] Everything can be inspired by Zen, as we can understand from this article.

In Zen philosophy the house obviously occupies a place of prestige, because it is the place where you spend more time and where you can recharge the energy that modern times take us away. Transforming your apartment into a corner of tranquility thanks to Zen principles will lead you to think more clearly and to better face everyday challenges.

Furnishing the house according to the Zen philosophy means creating a simple and orderly environment with few furnishing accessories, with essential lines. Always choose furniture and organic products - wood must be the king of the house - The lines to choose are square, clean and essential and with few decorations.

https://donnad.prod.h-art.it/a-casa/casa-e-arredo/interni/filosofia-giapponese-zen-cos-e-e-quali-sono-i-principi.

[49] Master Tetsugen Serra, op. cit. pp. 205-206.

[50] Cf. Master Tetsugen, op. cit.

[51] Someone will be surprised by the zen-martial arts approach, but here is a step that explains their relationship well: Zen in Martial Arts.

Zen in the Martial Arts has achieved a prominent place, particularly in the art of the sword and archery. Technical skill in combat is worthless if it is not accompanied by an inner tranquility, by a vigilant spirit that does not stop anywhere.

As the Zen monk Takuan said (1573-1645) "The true spirit is like *water* and the broken spirit is like ice", that is when the spirit stops on something, like ice on a branch, is bound and unarmed, when it is like water, there are thousands of possibilities and roads.

With the practice of Zen we arrive at the dimension of "exploded time", that is, in a dimension in which events are something detached and seem to be filmed in slow motion.

In combat the most ancestral instincts emerge, the deepest part of our being, and Zen through meditation allows the subconscious to rise to the surface. In this way one gets in touch with oneself and gets in tune first with one's own spritito, and then with the universe and consequently with the adversary. Perhaps with this Haiku that follows you will be able to help you understand this concept:

> *The water of the Hirosawa pond*
> *Doesn't think about reflecting the moon,*
> *nor, for its part, does the moon try to be*
> *reflected on the water.*

That is, there is only one moon in the sky, but the surface of each river reflects a moon. If there is no water, the moon will not be reflected, but water does not create the light of the moon. The moonlight does not change if it is reflected by many rivers, nor does it change its size.

Our spirit does not have to worry about the things on which it rests, just as things do not have to notice the presence of our spirit (http://www.rico54.com/zen/).

[52] The art of sushi preparation is an authentic Zen ceremony where the aesthetics of the composition and the preamble necessary for the pleasure of tasting.
(http://espresso.repubblica.it/food/dettaglio/lo-zen-e-larte-di-preparare-il-sushi/2061793.html).

[53] Spread over the centuries from India to China to Japan and then throughout Asia, it arrived in Europe, in France, through Master Taisen Deshimaru in 1967 and is now practiced and known throughout the world. (http://www.zenroma.it/zen/)

[54] http://www.zenroma.it/zen/

[55] Cf note 1.

[56] Citation of the refrain of the song "Holly and Benji" by the Gem Boys.

[57] Cf the book by Eugen Herrigel, "Zen and archery", ed.cit. (cfr. note 1)

[58] If you don't like the soccer-zen combination or it doesn't convince you, here is a golf-zen one , also inspired by the book "Zen and archery".https://www.caneogolf.it/psicologia-del-golf/zen-e-golf/

[59] http://www.centodieci.it/2018/04/come-essere-piucreativi-con-lo-zen/

[60] https://www.visioneolistica.it/contadino-saggio-storie-zen/

[61] http://www.centodieci.it/2018/04/come-essere-piucreativi-con-lo-zen/

41390023R00049

Made in the USA
San Bernardino, CA
02 July 2019